Learning Country

Sarah Tiffen

Learning Country
Song Cycles from the Heartland

Learning Country: Song Cycles from the Heartland
ISBN 978 1 74027 334 3
Copyright © Sarah Tiffen 2005
Cover photo: Robin Tiffen

First published 2005
Reprinted 2019

Ginninderra Press
PO Box 3461 Port Adelaide 5015
www.ginninderrapress.com.au

Contents

Dry Area: April	7
Little Towns	14
The Flat Country	21
Requiem	31
Back to the Farm	39
Casuarinas/The Presbyterians	46
This New Year	59
Autumn Is God's Season	63
Winter Solstice (2004)	64
Canberra	66
Changing Guard	67
Faith	69
Proof of Life	70
Blue (Hot Suburbia) I	71
Blue (Winter's Membrane) II	72
Departure From a Small Town	73
Farm Waking – 9 July 2004	75
First Day of Autumn in the Year of Fires	78
Learning Country	81
See to Believe	89

Dedicated to
my children, Tom, Lil and Wilbur
my parents, Robin and Jim Tiffen, Mum and Dad
my grandmothers, Eve Tiffen and Dorothy Harris

Dry Area: April

White chalk road cuts alabaster through red earth.
Groundwork of the Riverine.
Intermittent brown and yellow grass paddocks, places of scrubby pine –
Radiata, cypress, mounted amongst lichen rock. Dogleg gravel round the
Main Canal: the mother canal flows broad-hipped and deep,
Brown lodestar of the irrigated lands.

The glassy breadth of Douglas's storage dam,
At the Borderlands, succour of lucerne shoots, a single acre of
    salacious green,
The eye compelled by the flat sheet of tugged silk.
New forms of watering in the unwatered plains –
The experiment with the agriculture blokes.
Between its dug-up-turned-over banks, hills and sky captured in
    coppery brilliances,
A shiny metallic sheet of blues and browns and green, a mimicry
Of sea, billowed insouciance. That water! A true wet miracle,
    begetting grids of green,
Green, a green of God, that tidy green

From which we trundle, into the raffia-lands, into the
Dry Area. We are venturers to an older place –
Before water, before Sturt. Place of the outliers, place of remnant bush,
The endless fenceline.

Straight as a crow flying, by Round Hill, Square Knob out back there
    – the squat ramparts –
Walsh's sheds and the great gathering of equipment, Stony Point and
Lashbrook's slopes, Beaumont's small economy, Lewin's red-roofed
    homestead,

Pike's, McCormack's, the willow land, the clustered amber vineyards,
    the nestled places and
Old families, to the blue profile of the Bunganbils far out there, past the
Colinroobie. Remnant hills and blue, chipped off against the sky, the
    rough edge of
Broken china buried half in reddirt and worn off by rinsing light.
Far away, like a boy's broken glance, a sad heart angry, dontloveme,
Turning shame. The milk-blue eye.
To Blakella's untouched rocky brows,

The antipodean light, that White and High, that negative
Blinding haze, touched all over with a blanched gold, bleached red,
    that miracle light
Harsher and more unforgiving, truer and cleaner, blunter. That blank
    hanging enormity.

*

The ute shudders on gravel. Locusts in flittering swaths
Gentle oblivious and thickening, filtering through gold dusthaze,
Die upon the windscreen; tremble, stuck in their own juice,
Filigree ornaments the fender, the radiator.
Children's heads in profile beside me, hair caught aflame
In the same gold haze, the lengthening light.
Everything ridden with gold.

From a distance, I imagine we sail. Chalky plumes billow in our wake
To hang in stillness. We journey out from the irrigated gurgling land –
From the green.
Shadows grow from us, no obstacle in the flat land,
Till we are vehicles and figures on stilts,
The Minmi people and cars.

Here this sheer stillness, this silver glint of gums in slight afternoon
   breezes,
The eucalypt-oily sheen in light, clusters of spinking glomesh leaves.
A wintry metal light, dry sadness of pines, Sturt's vision here, the
   scrubby
Mangy pelt, godless to his green-hungry, rock-worn eye.

The small smoke signals of industry – tractor plumes – great clouds
Of rusty topsoil, here, here, here, round about.
Solitary beasts toiling the flat seam –
Great distances from one another but in communion, flung up and
   motionless,
suspended in April. From great distances, the bestial roar and rumble
Of colossal motors, tyres bigger than two big men, is quietened.
They move with a zen calm, ritualistic,
Ploughing from end to end and back.
Hail to the tractor, crafted iron, horse power, works ancient soil into
Meaning – fallow, furrow and row. Hail the calloused hands of men,
   working steel,
Working the great beast of the machine, as it snorts and roars
Into the great distances.

*

My brother's farm is mighty.
The barley stubble spread like sea to the edge of the sky.
Dense tufts, shifting like a yellow pelt.
Fenceline highways and sheeptrack lanes, rough streets of tyre-scored
   mud,
The dusty track that serves as driveway – five miles from gate to house,
Through stubble's leonine fur.

Sentinel pines, intermittent, tower above sweeping flatness.
To walk from the gate to the house, from the house
To the rise, across acres and into the mystery of unscathed bush there –
Rocky overhangs and moss caverns, cave markings, spirits – would
    take hours.
The size of suburbs, and all one great kingdom of soil.
Pines are witness-bearers, sheep-shaders, sea-parters from Cypress,
Their dry Grecian antiquity, dusty-scones-and-tea-picnic-invokers.
A sodseeder will scour around their base, but they hold the soil together
Ineffably, patiently awry.

*

A study in minimalism, amidst something vast –
Huge continuous tear of sky, vast knuckle of the hill,
Scree-slope with ragged bush, scrubby-ancient, land bigger than suburbs,
Bigger than racecourses or football fields.
Bush-sized, bigger than city hearts.

*

My brother.
Gentle, silent, tall as trees.
Strides each day across unbroken land,
Conqueror, pilgrim, incanting rain from waterless skies,
Wholly himself upon that earth and that stubble, scrub and soil
That are his kingdom, wholly his own. No man can
Rattle him, except the Father in rages,
With quick criticism, though women have at times.

Those unwitting city thugs who can't
Grasp the internal code of decency, common
Sense, hardwork no fuss, which govern here,
Are swiftly weeded out – dismissed. They don't rattle him –
He shakes his head, and restrains his fist,
Bigger than a melon when clenched.
A strong deterrent to any dickhead.
In towns, the pubs, on the footy field, driving,
At the sheep sales in Merungle, Barellan,
Griffith, working, walking about at the Show,
Or at the Field Day, or Ute Muster,
He is inconquerable.

But see, out here, he is master, and apprentice,
Brought to face himself. I imagine him, there, amidst
All space and solitude, the man alone.
He looks up from toil, from striding.
In wonder looking up suddenly, that silence
Ringing about him suddenly – that
Momentary comprehension of the enormity amidst which he strides.
Does he turn and face down
Eternity there in rock, soil, sky,
Sheer distance?
Does he, wholly himself and unobserved,
Drop down there upon the soil hard as iron,
His knees cut by stubble and unnoticed,
And hold his hands up to the sky, and balance there, beyond
All modernity, rendered small and spiritual, beneath the
Colossal presentness, sheer and mighty,
The Flat Land, the ancient climb of the hill?

*

A man can find equal distances in himself
Amongst such brown unfluid mass –
The unutterable distances of land meeting sky
At the furthest point, the horizon a far pendulum
Upon which the bloodsun swings.
Sheep tipped over and stiff, crows at their eyes,
A stark bale with dark godless sockets.

We may be steadied there, balanced on the
Rim of the washed sky, brought to reckoning
With each step, carving rows of ploughed sense
Into bleached earth. The dam is muddy and sacrosanct, luring ducks
And crickets to trill a bleating chorus
Incanting God from the rendered purple light
Twilight in the Dry Area, in the Colinroobie.

*

Tractors sail, galleons billowing topsoil –
Unspoken thoughts above vast paddocks.
The fleet in that wide ocean, rustic armada,
In the flat sea, in the ploughing time,
In the planting time, the work-it-up-out-of-the-desert-drought time.
In the April golden time, gold insect sparks illuminate
The gossamer-air, sweet-dusty-pollen-burst, dried-honey
Cluster time. Honeycomb impact. The locusts fly
Beautifully to fender deaths, radiator's metalsong
Hot lime smell, perished insect pung hung on prisms
Of gauzy light. Panels of brown yellowgold and white bleached,
Leached of colour, the mangy pelt of the scrubby hills further back.

*

So here on the first journey,
We stand, squinting into the sun, kicking dirt
Facepowder-fine and dark as blood. Contemplating enormity.
It is unavoidable and will be countenanced with each visiting,
The turning of the everyday. The silence demands it and its presence is everywhere.
No distractions, only in the hard pubs and wilderness of hot hairy Friday
Nights and in beds with warm flesh, and when the footy field crunches
Bodies closer and heat and anger are a panacea to
The Enormity.
We stand there, reduced, in the land without
Phone coverage, the land without streetlight, the land
Strung casually upon a vast fenceline,
The magnetic soil, no faultlines, reverberating
Songlines, colossal timelines.

*

The light in the kitchen is dim and cool.
The echo of china, kettles and tea. The peeling
Anchoring table.
A deep draught, and an outward breath.
At day's end.
Lifetimes woven into the soil.
Made intact.

Little Towns

Little towns slip away as we drive.

Outposts, gabled red brick and fibro colonies,
Gateways to the wide flat country,
Where buildings have one storey, two at most,
Stories pool in shady corners,
Behind staghorns, rubber plants,
Mother-in-law's-tongue, and other succulents,
In the shaded verandas, where clocks chime,
After church, after elevenses.

*

Trees gather to the roadside, leaving
The round hills stripped – a moulting pelt
Brown as fur and mangy, a scarified dignity
Undulating out and out in brownnesses, pocked
Rocky ancientness, sentinels craggy over
Arranged sheep dyed the dirt colour, soiled
Wool and grazing, still as pictures of wool,
Carved out of felled wood, bloodgum and tussocks.
The countryside assumes a broad azureness,
Flat stillness, hazy, holy and inhuman.
The road streams away in our wake as we plunder on.
Such gatherings of gums, textured like the
Swathes of lanolin fibres
Baled leaves and gossip-huddling, aghast
And whispering at our passing. The car
Draws them into our slipstream
Lured from the landscape to the roadsides,
Gatherings, ruched hems and edges.

The land in their wake is clearfelled.
Generations have been sustained by the clearing
And grazing, the stalking of cloven feet,
The steady mastication of ovine, bovine gums.
Nations fed. Economies buoyed.
Stretches of treelessness tell stories
Of high fine times and stateliness.
The girls off to PLC and boys to Knox,
Whilst the country brimmed with the fat of the land.
The Wedgwood chinks quietened, as topsoil sweeps away.
The little towns carry ghosts in the architecture,
In the stately roofs and porticos,
The Art Deco banks, and high churches.
Emptied out.

*

Little towns lure us along – Binalong, Bowning,
Harden, Murrumburrah, Kamarah, Wallendbeen,Springdale,
Stockinbingal, Pucawan, Mirrool, Gidginbung,Thuddungra,
Bribbaree, further out to Cootamundra, and the Great Sturt.
The song of names on the western path.
There at the great crossing, at the mighty turnpike of
Fourways – to the Newell, great rumbler of trucks and lives,
Or off to Wombat and Young, land of the cherrypickers, land of the
Sharrocks and far winters on horses, and by fires, and young
Reprobates.
Here the ancestral soil – my own blood lain down,
Lain beneath cracked marble under peppergums
And peppercorns – lush soil in the cemetery paddock.

We ate corned beef and pickle sandwiches
With the baby there, calmed by tombstones,
Oblivious, and unoblivious in the sun,
Our swift journey to them, lichen-stone whispered.
Cruikshanks, and Southgates, and broken hearts and
Heretics, and stoic settlers all.

Gentle bends, currajongs, jacarandas gracing corners –
Mirageous blue offered up in goblets
Hung up on coined branches beseeching the sky,
Then amid humble gums bottlegreen and lashed
With diamonds in windy winter sun. Cradles of rock,
Sad pines tall as hearts and courage, lonely giants
At the roadside and soothing in groves, and the light
Hung up on spires, brassy quenching light, flung up
As copper webs to glint wholly in hexagons of tears and
Swinging magpie dipping calls, and nonchalant currawongs
Shouldering a pendulum of birdnotes, arcing and swinging
Through parks and backways in
The Little Towns.
Where houses have stood still, for
A century and a half, twenty tides of birth and death,
Watched from awry verandas, and
The frank shuttered window ledges
In the small streets under gums and spires,
Back from the shops and the cenotaph. All borne witness.

Time framed differently, a different fumigation
Expunging from the earth as we stop to eat and
Stretch in the different dancing light.

Time more gathered, more flung, greater into older
Treetops, and knitted like blankets from
The threads of lives – calmed rhythm of soil
And sowing time, rolling out from
Quiet lives and houses, part-ancient, yet
Young deaths break hearts amidst the
Ordinary beauties – horsefalls, TB, childbirth,
Drownings, poisonings and common blights, colds
Ears, pneumococcal (then unknown) or cot death, when angels call
Early, that sweet nethersleep, God recalling souls
Without warning, or MVAs as they say,
The midnight car smash, and nervous copper's knock
At 4 a.m., the curse of the heartland, bright flesh in twisted metal;
Almost expected, but who will get got…
Death there in the willowlands and the farming grazing
Hilly miles, wayside chapels should be tucked there,
Imagined, dilapidated. Each death is recorded in the faces
And stone of the place, entwined and painful, communal.

Farming for generations
Can be like walking against the wind, lips thinned
Through pressing on, resilience, or doggedness, even when
The last stock die in the dry creekbeds and crows wing down
Hungrily, the sun is harsh heat and merciless.
Frayed edges, and peeling paint in the Little Towns.

*

In the wide streets, deep cool boothed cafés,
Woolies, the Tearooms, the CWA. Some quiet
Unreachable coolness in the Pub Majestics, The Royal,
The London, The Queen's Arms, The Grand. Gracious giants of
Architecture. Spiritual as churches, with huge verandas
And staghorns and treeferns round the rooms for let,
The bathrooms with baths like dams and showerheads from
The last century, big as hydrangeas.
The echoed fracas of every Friday night, when
Bodies throng to the dirt smell-glorious amber and sweat
Of paddocks and luscious smokey violence
Of boots, musky girls, huge outpourings of
Life force so pent up and roiling under the big sky all
Week – it all fills up the pub with its glorious sex and punch-ups
Ending in laughter and hugging mates and passing out
Between long country legs, asleep with tongues locked, and
The smell of earth in the back of utes.
It's a ritual in the pub cathedrals,
In the Little Towns, a purging of sins and
Spinning of webs, babies get made this way,
And mates give away sisters and get entwined
And related.

All but an echo in the still rinsed light
As we pass back from the twentyfirst century.

Streets widen to river width
And bracken and cicada smell, and the architraves
Encarved with old numbers – 1842, 1816, 1887. A
Long time brooding in the scrubby land, away from
Highways, American franchises, only antique

Shops, Art Deco theatres and the rose-trimmed
Colonnades of tearooms, federation awnings –original –
And the thistle-ridden wastes between sinewy
Railway tracks, sidings and silos.

What quiet life within the houses there.
Yards back up to the sky and dogs
And machinery and tyre swings and stoic
Lawns – couchgrass watered from the
washing machine, and curtains like whispers
of longing in the frayed windows.
Faces turn to us as we pass: they are neither
Curious or suspicious, but open and proud –
Faces of County Cork, Manchester, Carnarvon,
The Isle of Wight, the East End once –
Ruddy, freckled faces, or the dark ones,
Or the pale Norse ones, all tempered
By the light, by time, into Country Faces.
They note our passing through – we are foreigners,
City-dwellers, bureaucrats, artists – we are outside
The rhythms of the little places, we could be
Anyone.
Boys in utes wave, their youthful hunger makes them
Playful, forward. When we pull in for juice and fuel, quiet plain women
Behind shopcounters venture a smile. I smile back –
I have the face of a country woman – open and
Freckled. There is a rhythm in my heart that matches theirs
From the past. They insist – no pretention, no airs,
Empathy, self-effacement, low drama, hard work. Their husbands
Might carry some electric – the hard body of a physical life,
The light of careless intelligence – nice teeth, big hands.

I look at them curious and distant.
Envy the women – the nestling solidness of them.
Pass on, touched by them.

*

Stopping after miles of the gravelly roar, that
Endless driving of mile upon mile into
Straight distances. Ardlethan in its reverie.
Patient, staunch. Loud silence as we sip tea and
Stretch and breathe the peppery dust, the
Cockatoo-and-galah-air, the peppercorn immensities.
The Community Hall solid in its corrugated iron
Walls and echo of footsteps on floorboards, coy
Girls and the silent men who speak only to the dirt and sky,
The beasts, except Saturday nights. A world away.
Incubated from the pulse of cities, the breathless matrix.
But facing down the giant sky, the harder mistress earth,
The great inhuman distances. And fibro houses called
'Dunromin' or 'Thislldoo'. Dusty filtered light, sweet
afternoon beer, resilience, resistance and resignation.
In the Little Towns.
We pass on through, seeking Barellan,
Blakella, the lights of the irrigated towns,
Roaring into the West.

The Flat Country

Out in the flat country, in the wide
meniscus country where the lens
bulges back against the sky.
The clatter of tracks, bluemetal
railway stone sinuous steel
tracking grids through paddocks as green as the
lawns of the Parliament,
rice paddies, green as limes and
hustling there snakeslither in flat country
breeze.
Out there where men steady themselves
on two feet wide apart.
The world rocks and curves
so close to the sky, and the sky
so wide, swelling and cupping the earth there
like a bearing greased by oily orange sun
and rinsed by light.
The curve of the earth is there and
must be gripped.

Those men tall as trees and
quiet, smelling of grease and soil,
folded arms like the legs of sheep,
colossally muscular, bristling with ginger hairs.
They talk without moving their lips out there
and mount the rim of the sky
in a steadying of Blundstones
facing down the sun.

Standing on the surface of the earth out there
west of the twenty-first century,
back into heartlands of nineteenth century lore,
of twentieth century rituals,
a pastoral place
just a few hours from Sydney
but worlds from there, or anywhere,
but the heart.

*

Standing on the surface and
looking up to the bottom of the sky
a glassblue underwater feeling
Steady your feet, Jimmy Tiffen, Greg Tiffen,
McCormack and Pike and Duffy, Beaumont and all the rest
Hermanns in their own Deutschland; Robertsons, Scots
and lanky with their dark wild hearts, and Irvines,
Bradshaws, Bully Heiffer, fierce Walshes:
cousins and bloodbrothers, with folded arms and
the understated nod of heads,
coils that loosen and fling out
unravelling bales when
the circle of men is gathered and adorned
with glass and amber, in the shadow of the beer garden.
Then their voices lasso out into
jokes, weather, rugby, women, prices, harvest, the juices of women,
the weight of the weather, and the fucking government
and city dickheads,
and later blood and fists,

and in the morning a steadying sweat in the paddock
and more beers after the harvest,
and church for some and the shadow of the hungry sky
for the rest.
Steady at the fenceline, boys.

*

At the fenceline we could balance there, and then backflip
into the hugest blue enormous depths
of the washed-out sky,
the oceanic sky, the frightening massive canyon of
Sky.

*

Out there the land is still a colony.

English lads coming out for centuries to build a life
of mechanics, space, freedom, brown water, gung-ho and private,
and lace their nuances of the North and Yorkshire and other shires,
and rugbytalk and beertalk and farming,
into the saltbush bleached crowsquawk, galah-twilling
cockatoo toofaraway haltertalk of the bushfolk out there –
that bastardised celtic lilt
flattened and sharpened by light
pommy with Koori, Yorkshire into Wiradjuri,
flat nasal jabbing and yawling
country and westernwhine and
short-breathed, in the seasoned heat
rank with pepper and dust.
Too hot to talk or breathe.

Some interlaced again with
inner threads of the immigrants, the Italians,
their broadvowel, heavy 'As', striner than strine,
garlic-and-vineyard orange-orchard bright and
lively-eyed softolive skin and gesticular
staccato –
intersecting the flatcountry tongue.
Out there where the colonies are still,
and local boys and girls too
go to England and Africa for a year or two
and feel at home with the exodus and fluxing flow
of young people between the far world and the old
not so long since the first English
stepped down from the gangplank into
this dreamtime, so foreign –

Where time is slower, in suspension
it is still the colonies,
all Irish and English
and Scot, Baptist, Presbyterian, Catholic, Church of England –
the towns shaped by the spires of churches.
The freckled skin and red-haired big-boned
turn of mind and the silent ones
and hovering ones and the shindigs and
singalong bushranger colonial wildness.

Still half-hanker
for northern climes; a bestowed half-memory of English
green and grey they have never seen, and are not aware
of longing for. Skin freckled, and freckled again and
then the freckles burnt away over the time
of facing down the antipodean sun, relentless, fruitful,
bleaching the world and hearts and hair,
bleaching the rhythms of mothertongue to a
nasal economy of breath and rugby pride.

Out there where the psychedelic hum
of cicadas up at Blakella through
dappled light and ragged ancient gums
colonial eyes see the oily seer sun
heatsmell heavybreath and pepper
of gums and bark and the vast
hypnotic thrum of the alien bush
in midday heat, it never stops
roaring, thrumming anciently
confounds the colonial mind, and
calms it, shapes it –
stand steadying in Blundstones
folded arms like legs of beasts.
Fed on beef: beef as sweet as dates
and tender, rich with stubble and grain,
and women's eyes crinklyfarsighted
from horizonscanning, no sea views,
but the utter mystery of landwithoutend,
and oceans of hustling grain.

*

In the flat country, in the wide
meniscus country, the lens bulges back
against the sky, the clickettyclack
of days and the tracks like a sudden
thought, sleepers and bluemetal stone
iron thick as saplings, polished to fierce
smoothness by the roar of trains
the immensity of them, the weight
and sheerness of their thunder.
From Sydney, freighting the century
behind, and the roar brings sudden
thoughts of there, of other places,
and bent heads in windowframes
with the air of the future around them,
white skin slim limbs and the colour and
style of a future time,
the twenty-first century.

The city without boundary,
the ancient Sydney embroiled in
spices and mosques and money like steel.
Balmain, Blues Point and Woollahra
wrapped in nets of blood and habit to
the milesaway west, colonial
but sophisticate, country cousins
cashed-up and folksy, make the
Ascham girls laugh condescendingly, and
coquettishly, make the Scots boys laugh
scornfully, then teach them how to shoot and ride
and roughen up their caféhands,
and nests of blood and bone forged.

The-sister-married-the-realestate-agent-PottsPoint-,
and-the-cousin-in-importing,
or-flying-and- in-the-merchant-bank-
we-grew-up-together-at-Bega-where-the-dairy-was-money-in-cheese-
my-father's-father's-sister-was-his wife's-
mother-we-had-holidays-at-Jervis-and-Palm-Beach-they-had-
money-they-came-out-to-the-farm-a-few-times.
Habit and belief tie them in,
but a world away a world away.

Sydney, Sydney, the Rocks and the Bridge
like sentinels to the past, barricade the glitter
and murder, the white buildings
and the beautiful terrible harbour,
too much traffic and people too close
together, people self-actualising;
the air seems brown faraway but oilylimpid close up,
it never stops roaring,and
trains trains bring the roar of
that foreignness six hours away to the Flat Country
and in the same state! but faraway.

And then back go trains with colossal densities of
wheat groaning in each truck,
a mile of them together, yawning along the track
spinning off forever into the immensities of sky and
paddocks without end only steelwool tangle of fence
and grey fenceposts
out of mulga.

Fences out here are irony,
little punctuation marks,
a faltering hieroglyphic
of modern man, and somuchsweatandmoneyinfences –
thousands!

The trains spinning off from
the edge of the world, a country
offering to the bright century
a dull shuckettashucketta waverolling roar
round the unseen Murrami bends
where Bob Robbie went down –
it broke many hearts out the StonyPoint
way, by the Main Canal,
Colinroobie foothills,
and Murrami all over, by the siding and silos
backed up against the rocky hills and scrub,
against the sad angelic blue of the
autumn sky, the dull train snaking in through
deadly mist, and they still live there
and the train goes by every day
his missus and the boys they hear it
and it patterns their dark dreams
with the seemingly innocent
familiar shuckettashucketta
hiss and rising roar, no lights or horns in the
blank fog, only sirens
and shock shock shock from a light mistake,
breaking their hearts without reason into
their manhood,

into their dotage
weeping under peppercorns older
than ages
and a lone crow drives boys to drink
and sex with its lonely lonely
mocking craw.
The hoarse call of the train from beyond the mulga
the sinuous turning of the liquid track
round blind bends –
look out for the train –
it hurtles through from Griffith, from Sydney
through Junee and through Narrandera,
through the little sidings, through Yanco and
past Murrami, Yoogali, all the way through to Coolamon
Corowa…
old-time transport, sedate,
sudden reminders of loss
and the world beyond the
magical glass of the sky's eye, and
of the future never catching them.

*

Out there
in the flat country
God watches curious distant
then looms in with wizard's breath
to take up the sky
to herald days, and bless
the hardy colonials.

The world rocks and curves
so close to the sky, and the sky
so wide, swelling and cupping the earth there
and rinsed by light,
the curve of the earth is there and
must be gripped. Those men tall as trees and
quiet, smelling of grease and soil,
they mount the rim of the sky
in a steadying of Blundstones
facing down the sun.
Standing on the surface and
looking up to the bottom of the sky
a glass-blue underwater feeling.

At the fenceline balancing there,
between credibility and archaism
and then, and then,
backflip
into the hugest blue
enormous depths of the
washed-out the oceanic sky
massive canyon of the sky
of all things passing in their own time.

Requiem

Far out in the western sky,
Beyond Stony Point, beyond Murrami,
Past Jerilderie silos minted coins stacked, and
Calorafield, past the Brolga ground
And Old Man Pelican in the Broken Trees Place,
The Swamplands, gravely sitting there,
Above Whitton,
The scrubby river country, unutterable distances
Of land and grass, of broken trees, and the brown, brown water
  flowing –
A new star has appeared.

Large and bright, nonchalantly shining,
It beams down big and bold,
Divine in its solidness, its
Arch beauty and simplicity,
The big new star.

Beneath the shining palette
Of that sky, its billions, and its new star,
Beneath the great canopy of sky, stand young men.
Wearing their armour of grief,
Wearing stoic robes of courage, of staunchness,
Trembling slightly, assuming the warrior stance –
Feet wide, in a circle loosely,
Hands agrip a green can or
Brown bottle, workboots thick
With the grime of paddocks,
Workshops, beasts and blood – the earth that
Offered them up and before which
They stand quietly, looking into
Middle distances, and the sky, looking into the ground,

Reverent of delicate balances, reverent of their
Own failings and fleetingness,
Of the lore of death and growing things,
Reverent before the New Star.

Their voices are like the murmur of rivers,
A deep chorus of undertones,a gut-deep moving
Of country sound up and down, and drawn out
Pauses and stone sounds and the earth in their throats
Earth murmuring gentle and gravely,
Chainlinks of words barely spoken,
Linking them.
And then the broken shudder of a
Man often-silent,
Crying,
With his face awash and
Shoulders hunched and shaking,
Shouldering the immensity of grief
And sky and the heavy loads of
Manhood and silence out there.

And then other big hands
From the circle of their grief
Reach out, come down on
A shoulder, a single pat held firmly, and
Grip at the bones and blood
of brothers there – the great musculature
of hand,
A gesture of silent love,
as deep as the earth and sky,

And then to the circle of grief
There in the warm light of
The country pub, beneath
The endless darkening of sky
And the rose blush of dying day across
The ineffable west, across the village hush.

And the star beams down
Unflappable, benign,
And its beams hang there
Brightly above the road,
And angels and eagles flying high
Look down upon that ordinary road
A country strip of bitumen, no more
Or less, just a road…
But the twin streaks of black rubber,
Idiographic,
Turning against the straight grain of the tar –
To the side, mate! Mate! To the side,
Back up…and quickly

Quickly how the car
Leaves itself, its simple hieroglyphic on the road,
The rubber strokes of black.

Quickly, quickly in a bright flash does the
World fall away…

And in that one colossal moment
As long as a life of dreaming,
All life compressed
And present, in the blood and life of
That man aloft in the new world,
A king of worlds,
And the light and clenching beauty
Of all things is held there
Like prayer, forgiveness
Pouring through his body
Like a blessed rushing, like a vibrant seering
Joyous heat.
Never more in himself, in his own aliveness
Throbbing with the bright ecstatic fear
The deep believing
And the utter connectedness
To all things in that dark universe,

And a great call of joy
Uttering forth from somewhere outside himself
And the sliding slowly
Into that joy, slowest motion,
A last glance sideways to his fellow reveller,
The young man at the wheel, and a slow smile,
Seeing their Thursday night comradeship
In sudden eternity, never
Lost from each other for the rest of time,
The best night of all,
And then…a pause, a split moment,

For wonderment, at this magnificence
And the power of his great heart beating blood
Through his body and the world at once…
And away…

Up and away in a massive burst
Of ecstatic light, the
Car is sliced in two.

And God retrieves
His footsoldiers, the wild one
And the laconic one – the Big Man –
Who watched how quickly
And how slowly into the
Bright future and shrugged
And flew away lighter
Than a heartbeat
Into a million beams of
Light, and laughed
At the joke of it all,
Bemused at his sudden magnificence,
The orgiastic instant of his young death.

His body found fifty metres from the
Wreckage.

*

He watched them, surprised, casual.
Relaxed…yet concerned
To see the friends he left there
Friends he loved
On the gentle turning earth
The utter mystery of land without end,
And their courage and stunned
Silence, clasping on the rim of that
Colossal sky.
He felt a pang, to not
Reach out to them and say
'Yer bastards!' and laugh.

But eternity was warm and
So gentle, with the same gentleness
And deep placidity as a
Barstool in a cool dim pub
On any afternoon – in that flat country – a
Couple of punters, beer and the
Quiet static of footy from the telly above the bar,
A place of repose for the
Gentle friendly giant man
The decent open-hearted
Man, the humble man of no pretence.
'Don't mourn for me, me mates,'
He longs to quip, to rib them,
'Lighten up! Its fucken lovely
Here,' and laugh and scratch his belly,
At peace with the world.

But under the New Star of his
Bright soul shining out across the paddocks and channels,
Glinting on the silos, on the ghostly light
Of eucalypt, and across dumb animals
Grazing in blue light,
The men, those left behind –
So recently just boys, just boys –
Tall as trees and
Steadying the earth with
The grip of their Blundstones,
And steadying each other
With their arms of great sinew and muscle and bone
A warm hairy irongrip of love,
Are crying steadily
Without grace or favour,
Without shame:
'Drink up to the Big Fella!
Drink up to the BFG!
He's gone! He's gone!
Our Sinker, gone!'
And the words fall away
To think of that great living
Flesh and hulk of kindly
Man, gone…gone…

In a sudden flash of light, like a bright candle,
A beautiful thing, a gossamer thread,
Elusive
As truth, or love.

And they see, as they look about
That the innocent and simple-hearted
One, the pure one has been chosen first,
And are honoured
To have been in his presence,

And still anguished, anguished,
Hearts clenched and broken
All the days under the great sky
Out there –
For his loss,
For missing him
And their own blood beating
And love powerful
And the earth.

They stand in silence
And in awe,
Under their own bright star
Guarding them
From their own fragility
Watching them
An angel there
Far out in the western sky.

Back to the Farm

Back to the farm
where the days are empty
enough to reassemble thought.

Back from some twenty-first century psychosis
schedules pressed into our hearts
breathing feelings of pressing
of chests tightened
driving hastily and 'quick,quick!' to children
who don't want the lessons in
calisthentics; swimming; oboe; tae kwon do
days flicker with email, SMS, slick 'hi's'
always going 'somewhere', home days precious,
fretful; petrol-goes-up-on-payday-it's-a-scam-
Aldi-is-cheaper-but-not-Australian-made-
no water-for-lawns-cats-eat-natives-and-
there's-a-new-outbreak-of-pneumococcal-outbreak-
of-had-enough-living-for-tomorrow-not-now.
Worry; guilt; environmentally-friendly-it's-hard-work.

At the childcare centre, overworked underpaid women
smell desparate for recognition.
Suburb is empty empty on a weekday, a few mums
struggling with prams – she looks ragged. Joyous rambling
now stuck in childcare, mums don't play.
Sunday shutdown, and on sitting weeks, when the Parliament
is rocking, the bars are full of journos,
students, public servants making news glibly,
reluctantly.

Back from the fluorescent place to a different glare,
squint against the colossal sky.

*

I take the highway for an hour or so,
The Hume, through middle ground
humming in monotony grey tree-ridden scree-slopes
semis rumbling, then take the right turn off into the west.
Broken-down roadways and sidecountry, the Back Way,
I stop and start and have my thoughts
and tunnel through into the towns and
less-than-towns, the secret lives,
defiant of the city, the latest.
Squatting and spread verandas, hang-in-there
empty streets, women on corners with
kids scattering and prams and hats, and
striding men in moleskins, in Blundstones,
in flannelette, dogs on utes.
Streets have stock and station agents,
five pubs like brocaded museums, sites of wonder,
dim and cool with the history of fists and love
in those towns, fertiliser suppliers, and machinery,
a haberdasher, AustralianChinesefood, antiques.
Kids ride bikes lazily, shiftily, glare under freckles,
hair bowlcut, pageboy fringes over their eyes and no helmets,
out of the 70s, trawling for trouble
for mates rock a few roofs, set fire to a mailbox
make a billycart, get some hotchipsinpaper
chikorolls, play playstation, go out for sheep muster,
then watch Clint Eastwood or Van Damme,

ride out to the hills with dogs and shoot rabbits and
break through bewilderment boredom
the sense of life elsewhere, but little do they know…

Men in blue singlets and shorts gather in beer gardens
cool with staghorns and ferns, dim calm of the midday pub
ghosts of sticky midnights sloshed away,
this pub's been here since Johnny Gilbert's time.
They shot him down, when Frankie Gardiner
was a gentlemen ranger and fluttered the women
with the thrill of his sharpshooting
slim-hipped grace and danger
the gallant, the mustering ranging time.
Now descendants domesticated by war, taxes,
the government, regulation, stand quietly
smelling of diesel and grease and sheep wax
soothe themselves with monotalk, sipping,
eyes to the dust or the sky.

Straight on past Stockinbingal, Kamarah, Springdale,
Harden-Murrumburrah, where the French teacher
made a small France with grapes and daughters
the landscape fit for moulding to illusion,
Temora, of the wide streets, of the gracious houses
kids riding horses in the park and the mainstreet
thronging, statue of a racehorse vying with
the new Woolworths for pride of place, they come
off the farms on Saturdays to do the shopping
on Sundays to church
God keeps a close eye out there;
the paddocks and heat can be godless and
break a man.

Straight down to the Ardlethan turn-off,
lonely hills of tin, and the fruitfly bins,
and on to Barellan, with the Pub Majestic
and boarded-up shops and a flash new
stock and station agents, if-only-people-
would-shop-local-the-bastards.
Barellan women make most blessed morning teas –
lamingtons, teacakes, scones, vanilla slice and
all the creams and lightfluffiness and jams
and soft sweetnesses laid out in plentiful eggful
milkrich bounty on trestle tables at the Gun Club,
at the Church Fete, at the Street Stall,
never bought Germaine, Susan, Naomi any
bullshit-women'slib-lesbian-crap, blood still pure
Anglo, and cooking out on the properties where
the light is as fierce as anger, and the only smell
is the old antipodean soil and eucalypt and the hotbaking
ancient Wiradjuri thrumming air on the wide flat verandas
looking through squinting at the hugest
blue, the watered-down scratchy blue of the
summer-storm-coming sky and the oceans of bleached
wheat scolding and gossiping with the wind
hssssss hsssss and cooking like they never left
England, was it three or four generations ago and
roast beef, pudding, fry-ups, tea and cakes! cakes!
and scones and all the English cooking, flushed and
full and built like staunch verandas, like
Victorian furniture, thickset, ankles like fenceposts
flushed to their Anglican hearts by the heat
of the stove and the eating and Church all dressed up,
and flushed from the fear of the land

as it hums ancient metallic, the utter mystery
of endless red land and the fields of sinister wheat.
Those Barellan Morning Teas, men travel
for an hour to tuck in.

Through the tiny dry towns out there
back back from the city
to the places I fled once
and now haunt, looking for what's there
for me to find in another century
without flinching.
The woman I have grown into
envious at the women out there
on the properties, big-bosomed, eyes
all farsighted from endless horizon scanning
skin reddened from the light, only lippy for
church, the crude red a shock, and hips like saddles.
They are ruffled down and settled down and
nested like hens and some enormous raw comfort in their
huge thighs and arses like a load of grain
they haul behind and the backs of their
arms like straps of lamb and some comfort in
themselves, within them, bovine, earthbound, the kind
sensible selflessness, ability to handle emergencies,
ineffable, fully appraised…
or is it resignation, or just the unperturbability
of small minds under the endless horizon
counting blessings, or has loss and suffering
inured them, anythingforaquietlife, or is it
or exhaustion, or faith? Perhaps they are not content,
but broken, I can't tell, but dream,
and come back, back to find out.

Back through this past that changes little
the same songs on the radio as I edge closer
runtoparadise, chisel and then I switch over to
FM – the timeless airy violin lifts me up out of memory
and gentle poshvoices edify, elevate me out of dusttodust.

We swing through the Colinroobie, coachhouse country,
Wiradjuri bluetongue country, place of Bunganbil, lichenleached
big rock Rainbow Serpent time, colossal rocks with mossydripping
underhangs and stern godface outreaches
up there through the stoic pine and the giant pine and
casuarina, redgum and greygum and wax flower time
snakestalk and blue smoke campfire time,
breathless-with-wonder-time, rockscrambling
moss-stained, rockpainting time, dawntime,
in-touch-with-country place.
I recall and recall the future there.
Here are the blue mourning hills and roofs as high as
a terracehouse, one-storey homestead with eaves to the sky,
like a Sydney terrace, but no harbour view;
only the utter mystery of landwithoutend,
the oceans of hustling grains.
From up there
the grid of the Dry Area, the agricultural patchwork,
laid out at the feet of Bunganbil, ineffable
portions of brown, green, yellow, white, ochre, grey,
black cows tiny amongst stubble, like currants in dough
and sheep just faint smudges against the white light.

Back I go where only
exhaustion will take me where it is high time
and year's end – season upon season.
The light is bleach, the back paddocks stinging
and white from it, pure as acid and white it
carves into my face from squinting
into silence
into heat
the clods crack open in the midday and
birds drop onto banks from scorching

Here I am at last suspended between worlds
seeking forebears –
farmers, publicans, orchardists,
soldiers, immigrants, convicts,
artists and Baptists, cold comfort for the fatalists
replete before God, before the vagaries of land
and homesicknesses so deep they're forgotten.
And I repose on the veranda
to the smell of hay, and dung and the
sun falling spilling across purpling
paddocks like split yolk,and forget
the future and say,
'Ah, back at the farm.'
Old mysteries begin.

Casuarinas/The Presbyterians

Casuarinas I

Casuarinas stand about together
in the space between the car park and the oval up there,
before the tennis courts, and outside
the Youth Centre.
A piece of undesignated dirt;
a place to meet, share cigarettes and 'g'days'.
The dirt impress of bikewheels
trekking back and forth through the days –
the school days and the footy days,
the days of cars and lipgloss,
of girls in low white pants, boys in low jeans
calling out and revving up,
the bigtime days, the schooldays –
under Big Mountain sky,
down the Valley way.

These poorman's pines;
frayed, stoic, unarranged.
Huddled, expectant.
They ring with the old bushlight,
old winters: river hymns and
water ripples through their sound.
Brownly, hushedly.

Here the Casuarinas
a dozen or so called together,
agathering in cold glassy light –
aventurine, shifting
hexagons of bright cold colour,
like through wet lashes, half-blinded prisms.

Spring sun, late in the day – footy fever
highcalling duskyfilterlight; in
the mountainous air, the high cold
calling, boys voices on the oval
rough and hoarse with the rub and vim
of training. Caverns of
time and earth loom against the near sky
lately snow defied both there.
The sharp cold has softened in this
early September fracturing of seasons.
The hay time and the honeybrush time
hovering closely and goldly by.

The beerglass light moves around through the
Casuarinas, shifting and spinking,
weaving through the shimmy of
a thousand green needles, the soft
shagginess of the
Casuarinas, their picasso-esque,
misshappen unkemptness –
that womandignity in their togetherpatternness,
their country churchyard faded oldness
achingness, soft whispering and whinnying,
the gentle gentle light, the afternoon-slanting-through-
church-windows-light, the soft hazy Mountford Park light
the said and done light, the dying light,
and muffled needleness
and liedown slowly, movewithinme-ness.

The sound tunnels canals of my ears
a burst and spiral flare in my arteries – down to the
chest heave and stillness of me,
my broken cup, in there, still drinkable,
enamel chipped off loyally and
still facing out the world. The
sheer mystery and wracking secretness,
simplicity, gentility
of Casuarinas together.
Breathing and whispering in winds
a carpetting of gentle needles threading
in the air, the sinus-cleansing, bellyfilling
browstroking, earwhispering, waterfalling
whitenoise of their singing and sighing
their slight moving and rubbing,
noble, sad and sighing there
on that rocky nature strip.

Tuggeranong Valley, wide and dry,
pine valley, bighouse, Slavic colonnades
and clubland valley,
hale under the blue shelf of
the wild Brindabellas, the
ringing linocuts of blue back and back to the
final horizon – undulations
of blue, green, wild bush
and snowlight, rocky slopes and grassyhills and scrubby
hills, that powderblue that fashions into
royal blue far away, that antipodean
verisimilitude – awash the sad
pale light.

Casuarinas II

I watch and listen to the light and sighing:
they stroke me.
There is a waitingness in me –
the tired baby sleeps in the back,
and the car is a cocoon
from the twinking cold and the angry house
and breathless doingness –
but there is more in this exact moment,
suspended in the light,
expectant and released into the
branches, moving as though shaken by children.

It is the softshucketing loneliness of the
sound, the brushhoney soothing hush
softness and soothing shade and
humble fadedness, the churchyard
dryness and faded greenness of the
Casuarinas.
The ground at their feet is
carpeted in brown needles, fallen,
and turning needles, laid as rushes,
laid in a strange softness,
although quite brusque and firm alone,
together they lay upon one another,
soft as a bed
where we tried to lie down
once,
when waters as shallow and rippled as
long hair floating
bride Ophelia falling

the wide spread of the river
under mighty She-oaks
under sandy-lit She-oaks
the mighty river woman
the sighing, the womb singing
the arch of the incandescent afternoon
light, mudsmell, passionlips
hotburning sand-abrased breastpressing
brownwater slither –
the casuarinas bore me up
in their soughing and sighing –
unutterable peacefulness
in that needley white noise.
I stored it in me – to catch me up in
the later heavy days and frightened days.
Emergent soughing She-oak needles
falling and lying down
soft and silent,
the green cathedral of the forest
under them.
The unutterable hush of the
Casuarinas thronging by the weir
there –

So it hangs in memory from before that
Black Saturday we can't speak of.
Because no one warned us, not the government
not the people, THEY didn't tell us – go!
We can't speak of that upset – we trusted
the infrastructure so implicitly – and
just live our lives in thoughts and

principles, but of course Nature, in the
Hadian time, the redsky fallingaway burning
away horror time, makes our suburbs a frontier –
we are colonials again and no infrastructure
no nicety – just us and death, no warning.
These things remind us.

Once the spiritsoaring high rush and rising of
the wind in the casuarinas brought me undone
by the brown river
the unearthly hymning and hushing of
the gentle needles
breaking and soothing my heart at once.
Beauty distilled before me and
portent on the needlesoftened
rough river sand
ancient antipodean whisperers
rivernymph voices
oldtree incanting sighing
prayers for the river, the sky and
the mystery of the hills
craggy, overhung, unpenetrated,
and the rushing shallows of the Murrumbidgee
tannincoloured riplets in old sunlight
gold as beer, whippywind cool
hot summer dustyriver legends
of fateful meetings lulled and hushed under the
Casuarinas
the deep pine shade.

Now the January Terror
has razed these monuments
these sandy brownwater times, the mud
smell and pine and pepper of the gums
decimated by Fire,
still black and singed a year on.
The fires of the black black
Saturday, when the river burned and the
Casuarinas lay down silently before hot wrath
and the villages and
hamlets, and the bushfolk and the startled
roos and wombats were razed, and birds dropped dead,
razed from the sky, by the apocalypse,
the weird orange summer, razed razed
the fire hurrying from the Brindies
see God's ineffable rage.
Now my memories are tenuous,
cleansed by fire.

Ah but on this quiet day
the Casuarinas
in the Mountain-and-Lake City
the town full of citadels,
organic people and students,
economists, psychologists, bureaucrats,
politics and intellect,
Greenies and Catholics, refugees,
secret Croats, Slavs, Italians, Poles,
Lithuanians – all sheltering under the
mountains' rim, the green valley blue
cut horizon. Science.

All wonder and snaking of Parliament here –
the white geometric heart, the triangle of
Power – Parliament, the Library of Knowledge, the Court and Science
  and Art – is nothing
in the face of the old homes and mountains
the farms and the rivers –
the fire and snow, and the
bleak summer fear – the brownness
of the limestone plains.
The easylisteningness,
bourgie bearded, short-haired
small-breasted women place, the bike place,
In the time of the Ridge saving
and BillofRights drafting, in the
time of recovery and dizzyness,
uncovered blackness and quiltgiving,
marriage-dissolving and road-dying.
This mountain-and-lake city.

Amidst it trees making a harmony, a pact
compelling me – their soughing.
remind me of something
deep within.

The Presbyterians

They are the Presbyterians
staunch and stubborn
Faces into the sun…

church by the scout hall and by the bare land
with cedars and thistles, the walking
homeafterpiano land, the Currajong purplelight
silverside and lavender time, the face powder
curlers and brownstone time,
mint sauce, fresh buttered bread time
camphor and dencorub time.
Relish, lost baby,
and churchcraft time.

Not her church, but the
thin, tall church,
like a quiet man –
simple and austere
devout through frugality, cold wind –
humble and threadbare Scots, worship the sky
and the wind, and the dirt beneath them,
and industry, the nobility of industry,
of thrifty and darned times –
and huddled they tend to the ordinary
hurts and hearts
and sing highland hymns and
always in their quiet,
unpretentious dreams are their hearts
turned to the highland and heather
and the dark green hills and the
wild sea, and they are facing the
bitter spray from the North Sea
irongrey, and the memory
from out of generations

of pipes and a turn of phrase
a look of the eye and starchy
habits of the kitchen formed them,
pride and tartan formed them,
the dance of the kilt and the
twitching blackshoed feet of lasses –
Lewises, Macintoshes, McCormacks and
Robertsons, Sweeney, MacGuire, MacAuslan
and their red hair or the bigboned tallness
and quietness of them, and their dour
ways and wild dark hearts and whisky, and
kiddies and grandkiddies dancing lovely
in their little kilts about the swords
bagpipes call mournfully, strangely
across bleached paddocks and gumtrees,

and the huge southern
sky with its merciless eye staring down,
as though it were another world away and
the old ways and the old ones
were still here

Countryfolk She-oak,
Bottlebrush,woodenfloored-church-hall-
flower-show-tea-time-crotchet-and-
that-crinoline-and-courtshoes-
pearltime, in the Old Faces,
and the churchtime –

Here they are, countryfolk trees.
They recall for me, signal me the people with hats in hands
People ate dumplings quietly and corned meat –
and prayed in the Methodist church, in the Presbyterian
and the Uniting – well-lived
quietly churchorgan hillrambling worlds;
concernedly standing round
as though they
surrounded one bereaved, or hurt.

Flat country people, bigboned, widefaced
murmuring, tongue-clicking, with frowns,
patting shoulders with the large flat gentle hand
the callous-knuckled, dirt-stained, short-nailed, broad-wristed
Doing Hands,
hands that can twist wire, snap the necks of
birds, or kittens, handle a gun, or the carcass
of a beast, deliver a stuck calf, wrench out trees
and move rocks and steel collossally,
recall big silent men hovering quietly, not wasting breath
on words, struck deep and dumb by
the ordinary suffering of others, offering
an arm and troubled, stoic,
having faced down hardship countless days
but no less moved.

And these, the bigbosomed, flatfooted, widehipped,
flatcountry women, smelling of talc and
musk, permed and starched
but a broad warm bosom of comfort there for
the sufferer, the air of silent
conference,nodding,murmuring,

an unuttering empathy, salt-of-the-earth
the casuarinas
the stoic hesistant gathering of trees
in the valley of
the burdened Tuggeranong.

Casuarinas III

This day in this awkward
non-place, the stand of Casuarinas
Planted twenty years or thirty –
a smaller town, a one-mall
humpyplace, in the time of the old Parliament –
making casuarina-shade upon the bindyfractured
soft stony red earth,
cemetery-sad rocky ground, patchy threadbare daisies
stoically beaming up, humble, doggedly cheery
decently spreading there.
the humble trees and humble dogged blooms
and unprentradious soil
in the cold spinking light
and the trees moving together
and the sound of white felt
blanketheavy peaceful,
so reassured and soothed by
the soughing sighing needles
and cones, small as grapes and
textured.

The Casuarinas gather
like folk after church, stayers gathered
after service for gossip and tea
in Wedgwood faded,
whiskery faded women
redlined lips and grooves,
pants pulled high to waists
disappeared in other flesh.
Magpies rinse out the sky with their call,
pay homage to the ordinary beauty of the trees.

This New Year

Outside it is 42 degrees celsius.

The air-conditioned house is a capsule.
The light in the garden seems
lucid polaroid, false greens
facile blue and white,
ostensible coolnesses.

The sky through the branches
of fertiliser-fed gums, plums and ash –
all redolently well and watered –
is opalescent blue
deep as a harbour, glistening
in blueness, vertiginous in absolute
mysteries of blue, blue, blue.

Faint movements in leaves and
garden beds suggests breezes.
Sea could be over there behind the shed.
The air could be edged with an afternoon southerly.

The irrigated colour is
seductress, impostor.
From the air-conditioned miracle of the
house humming its deceiving lightness,
the cool look of the green light
in the watered garden – these coolnesses doubly imagined.
Conspiring to elicit disbelief in this
January. Displaced hearts
almost beguiled by
Illusions of Green,
longing from somewhere in.

*

Celtic and Saxon hearts,
exiled seven generations from the
Highlands – still harbour the lakes and greyswept
wilding greenery and dripping dells
and moors, a hunger deeper than grief,
released through blood like a virus,
passed to descendants, longing for rain and
the muted tones of the mother isle, so long away.
The strange antipodean light and red dirt distances.
A kind of exile.
Hard-won, they have grown into the light,
cutting swathes through paddocks,
and across ovals for the ball, drinking
beer and shading their eyes from the light,
on beef, the felling of great trees, and the slow grazing
of a million sheep,
clamping their lips against the droughty
grit and flattening their vowels to nasal
twang and more silence, and
riding the rim of the sky in their boots.
They have grown big, a kind of evolution, to
shoulder the loneliness, to fill the
enormity of Space, the enormity of Heat, out here.
And build green gardens in
defiance of the simmering air,
to soothe the sense of foreignness.
After centuries.

*

This heat, this January, is
colossal, vast, weighty.
It cannot be resolved or denied.
It has the magnitude of
a Great Visiting. A Force. Almost fantastic –
Heat.
Roads dissolve and water turns to syrup in the face of it.

The signs of it are subtle from here.
Detect a certain
whiteness in the light
where green is turned to the negative,
obliterated in some atomic flash,
my eyes blinded by the secret whiteness
out beyond the yard.
Notice dogs under creepershade
pressed against the cement cold of the watertank
in holes dug out under the cold dirt there,
or one or two magpies,
usual heralds of crispness,
lost on the burning lawn,
beaks awry,
the strangeness of them sat there and
panting in the gelatin stillness.

Beyond the gate,
beyond the small oasis of the watered lawn,
another universe. If I lift my eyes beyond the green vista at this window –
the whole earth and century,

the Western Continent is baking
the new year baptised through eons by a sun without
prejudice, or mercy –
patient and unswerving in its duty
to heat us.

*

This is no England, no winter, no coastal isle.
This – the third day of this new year,
this Southern Interior
as it was always
and will always be.
This stillness and this heat
ungodly, unhuman, fearful,
wracking and steady.
Fifty years before this
houses baked full of dust,
and many perished or descended into
hell. Women in farmhouses
stared into mirages, desperate,
with such vicissitude.
And no relief at hand.

*

Almost inconceivable.
As I, in my sweet cold cocoon,
look out at greenery.
protected by modernity.

Autumn Is God's Season

These days have an internal rightness.
Les found the word – 'equanimity'.
Completed, and replete; air
Bell-light, free, chiming, mild,
Cathedral sky in meditative blue
A breeze on greenness, the last of
April praying gently, earth murmurs
And crickets, comfortable birds, calling
'Cockatoo', and some notes and happy
Bellbirds, currawongs willowing under
The pine and gum rush. It's the afternoon
Magpies warbling rightness. That captures it.
Quiet suburb and good air
Blows my hair, my heart and belly.
Encased in languid
Sun. Poised, resilient. These days.
The Brindabellas like water against the sky,
Liquid soft, erases red summer with azure
Undulations.

Winter Solstice (2004)

Snow across the Brindies
Powderspill on the heavy ancient brow
Dark blue creases in the velvet cloth of distance.
Cathedral sky weighted, bruising
Grey and other blue, sheet metal.
City folded down under darkling light.
Air succinct with cold,
Freezing crystalline.
Canberra murmurs its winter secretly.
Lights in windows are altar candles,
Eyes alight in the liquid glow.
Hearts beat somewhere,
Synchronistic.

Now is the waiting time
And the quiet introversion.
Thoughts like breath, sweet,
Low and hot. Longing pools
Within.
Seeking down and in, on
The shortest day, to old poems
Fragments of prayer, stained glass.
Still.
Dark.
Winter bone and brass.
The car park is like an etching – grey
Upon grey upon grey, challenging
Various shades of almost blue to bloom
Like spores, miasma.
Two-dimensional image of still cars.

I walk through still air-cold gelatin,
Solemn as death or love.
Streetlights are fish in the dark net of
The winter deep.
In the morning the dripping
Tap will be a stalactite.
I watch from the window,
Alone, the frost,
Earth hard as iron.
Heart fibrillous.

Canberra

The soft purse of the hills folds down
In darkling green and velvet blue
The air coddles into the nape of the
Hilled horizon, a dark green hush, pooling down
Into pure dark.
The sky is awash with diamonds
And the city purrs,
Small rivers of light and muffled
Sound.
On the hill, the Parliament stands
Like a citadel.
In the suburbs swathed in blue eucalypt,
Folk scratch and think out their lives;
Catholic, intellect, socialist,
In the shadow of mountains.

Changing Guard

Mid-autumn, before 7 a.m.
And the light across paddocks,
The garden and flyaway sky,
Pours from the furnace freshly molten,
Pure and gold,
Heartbreaking, and all
Greens illuminate in the face
Of the rising light. The day
Stirs. Brisk wind gathers the crowd,
Works them up – trees,
Leaves, birds – dart and stutter against gusts
Clouds called in, darning the
Rippedtorn sky, hazy milk-blue behind the
Threads and patches and unsolid
Wisped white.
A portentous guard changing
Unstill gums, melaleuca, peppercorn and
The wild plum, orange's plastic dark green gloss, claret ash,
The silky oak's clusters of amber tapioca,
Wild whispering willow-gossip, supplicate
Run and tussle with rising air –
A turning into day;
Winter gathering its forces for a
June assault,
Hearts fly up.
Cows cruise nodding through
Glittered paspalum, peewees
Report 'Sing up! Sing up!' Dogs
Perk up-ears up, nostrils flared, tails thumpthump,
On the ready.

All molecules charged. Insects, dogs, children
Gleeful, and birds girded for harvest –
All heady with the change, scented air,
Faint odour of winter, but first –
The Harvest Festival drawing crowds from the farms and
Back Ways, into the Main Avenue,
Into the Past.

Faith

(picnic with Tom and Lil in Weston Park)

The lake like blue satin
Cormorants sleek flit sends corrugations
Out like a pulse
Mole and Rat in the rushes, a gentle breeze
Under gentle sky rills the sheeny surface
Old pine, wider than three armspans, a
Gnarled sage, smell of peppers and
Soft needles, leans over us
Benevolent shade on the grassy bank.
The Brindies like a blue memory
Beyond the Governor-General's house
A white cockatoo swings like a pleasant thought
Across the midview.
My children, bright and sweet, and
Grinning and loving, seeking the
Sun, throw stones from the water's edge,
Lake sprites, beachcombers, harbour masters,
Waifs.
We sit on the rug and eat grapes and bread
And remember peaceful things
That we will do in the future.

Proof of Life

I looked back over the precipice
turned my lonely eyes to the sky
and found good reason there
arched back like a lover
I drank rain in the back of my throat
I was wet
sluiced in the thronging beads
my hair
hanging perpendicular to my head
I rode back like a rodeo queen
I rocked to the rhythm
of the stone to the
rhthym of the earth
murmuring deep caverns of time
driving up through the soles
of my feet like nails
my lonely eyes
heard the soulful lonely
sound of crying
my own soul
brought forward in the light
to find reason there.

Blue (Hot Suburbia) I

Still night and the moonlight like
washed silk, unholy, wholly undark
a voiceless blue world
silence rendered by heat, and the
webbed mystery of moonlight.
No leaves move
held in the dark gelatin of heat.
Still dark shapes in the dark blue –
trees; poles; roofs; fences; wires; sheds.
Dogs bark out, unnnerved by the
stillness, the silence, immense; by the tension –
between bodies, flung out sleepless,
strung on heat's wire,
dogs gulping rasping, the unhuman staccato.
It is the end of the earth
and we make shrouds of sleep
dreaming that order and sense may
be redeemed in the light, an
imagined fragrant cool.

Blue (Winter's Membrane) II

The night's cold moonblue –
out the window, the lonely blue street,
lamps like thoughts left there
in damp rings of bitter orange.
Jacaranda flails weakly against eerie blue air.
Cars roll by like stalkers;
other houses dull opaque,
iced in shadow.
The silence is vacant, no vibration of
cluttered lampwarm lives.
The landscape of this night,
like that future moon making the dark
milkwashed, drained of the subtle warmth of
true ancient dark.
Time, the stood-up lover,
resigns and pulls the darkness down,
sends me away into dreams of loss, loss…
I panic in blue cloudseas
waking up thirsty and
all my tears dried up,
feeling the cold cold blue of the drowned,
of the damned.

Departure From a Small Town

At the train station
Echoes of a hundred steam engines,
Shunted steel, ghosts of departures
In the fluted wood eaves, the old times,
The hiss up the empty track, last call of
The mournful whistle through rivergum
Dappling Land – like a vestige of woodsmoke,
Haunt the empty platform,
Neat and swept.
The bus arrives,
From off the Griffith road,
Hydraulics roaring.
And in the churn of the motor
Saying 'quick, hurry, no time'
Parents load sportsbags, old suitcases,
Packed sandwiches, books, sweets.

A last sweep of the flat dirt car park –
The railway lines a bright ribbon into
Lonely sky; the Mill, quiet in the early light,
Little row of houses, like a clump of mushrooms
Between the cattleyards and Felix' Joinery,
Dung and wood, the small town morning smell,
Parkview and the great canyon of the railway bridge.
Kisses and scuffing the dirt.
From the window mouthing 'Bye', 'I'll ring',
'Love you'.
Mother in a tracksuit, creased with sleep,
Hair unset.

And Dad, in his workclothes, flannelette and jeans, boots
Still muddy, and the stain of axle grease
In the grooves of his big hands.

Through prisms of brokenheart light,
Fading smaller and smaller,
A hieroglyphic of parent –
The source –
And they turn away, back to the car,
Arms folded.
The face in the window lost
To the glare of the sun, the one-way glass.

Magpies offer small heroic tributes
Of warbling, to unwept tears, in the repeating silence.

Their backbreak pays for the
Separation, for the university,
For the passage into the long days
Of longing, of silence.

Farm Waking – 9 July 2004

Back in the early hours, the flat paddock poised.
A cast of thousands – still shoots anodised, the
mercuric predawn sheen.
Still, still, not a quiver – a frieze of
paspalum, dead gums, peppercorns
hunched oldman colossal and crouched
counterpoints the brushstrokes of egret, ibis:
idiographic, Japanese.
Wiradjuri moon, the great melon,
passes out the hill gate, unhuman
light distilled into grey mourns
the black man, master of this rising,
worshipping for eons.
Now, the old farmers, thumbnail-sketched
on a pelty agri-canvas, paddock and
channel, cropped and raked,
the weighty daubs of earth and dung.

*

Watch as the conqueror mounts the rise,
unheralded, stealthy, but for the subtle shifts of
bare light, metal into blush,
heavy crystalline silence.
Then…

The dull thump of dogtails in dirt,
link against link of the restraining chain,
lifted slightly, a twitch, bracing.
Out of mighty stillness, peewee
and starling, a friction of feathers, fractions
of sound as minute as insects

scudding on irrigated fields.
A drawn breath, deep earth inhalation;
the sky anticipates with pearl.
It builds.
Chooks begin in the far pen to scratch
the mulchy dirt, quick then hesitant,
in their graceless, focused way,
and the air suddenly picks up the irrigated scent –
mud, wet, dung, green and
the tides rushes back, drawing sun
defying the shut purse of the Colinroobie,
and splits!
Like broken yolk streaming staining
ribbons and rivers of green and gold across the yard,
the dirt by the sheds, the house pasture,
everything submitting to molten light.
Sentient beasts wait, tense,
bovinely philosophic about this coming of day.
Each as if it were the first. They smell it, flexing
their great nostrils, sense it in hides. Snort
and stamp in steam.
Pods of ducks shoot from the dam's bow,
slingshot blurs from out of the kabungi.
A bark.
A rise of air.
A roil of warmth on the mist.
Kookaburra sees the absurdity, and
can't contain his jackal scorn, shoots off
his raucous hullaballoo from the ragged gums.

Away!

*

Inside, the scrape scrape of the woodstove ashes being emptied,
steam from the teapot rising, the smell of vegemite.
The men pull on gumboots at the back door.
The house unfurls chimney smoke.
Dogs, unleashed, now pant with base joy,
licking each other, mucal glisten.
The day lays down its lore.
Each singular sound merges and jams to become
The Morning Song
of farmers' wives, freckled children riding bikes,
calling cattle. The radio hints at
good prices for stock and fertiliser, footy scores –
Whitton Crows trounced the Yanco Dogs –
and lists of the day's dead.
Alan Wallet makes his broad-voiced
laconic statements, and the pan sizzles
with offal, eggs, thefatoftheland.
At breakfast, 9 a.m., they plan the day's business,
discuss the weather, free trade, roads and tariffs,
cattle sales, detainees, and Iraq,
Howard on the wane.

First Day of Autumn in the Year of Fires

Goosebumps today
sprinkling up the back of my arms
like ants scrabbling.
That warm, well-slept feeling under
a warm doona, no breathlessness
from a night of heat, the cool
morning, clouded, grey and steely.
Revel in the pewter light,
the wintry outlook over the hills.
Glory to the smell of rain!
The fledgling green!
It seems only yesterday…

I take in Mt Arawang
so close there in the watery light,
just right there, a few streets back,
a small walk with the pram
it seems.
just some rows of trees, a strip of sky,
and there it is, anomalous, sodden, sombre.

Brown and black now, a midden, a burial cairn,
round, unsightly, sheared of all
but one or two blackened broken shards of tree.
How welcome even that sullen brown,
that bareness.

Once upon a time the mountain was a
vivid demon of orange, yellow, red,
the fiendish crackling, the roar, the sour
furnace of rusty smoke pouring
utterly pouring
the dark apocalypse. Everything left scarred.
Our hearts.

After this summer no longer tastes
of watermelon, chlorine and
wet, sweet evenings under sultry skies
smelling of grass or ozone.
It is forever more – smoke, and a deadly heat
that drove us inside the house.
Dusty, smoky, ugly, frightening
summer to be endured…
Was it true? Did we nearly burn down?
and those people that we
know, from school, from soccer, down
the shops, on the bus, at the fete
or street stall, church or the 'Iro',
the baby health clinic, the bank?
Did they face death in the cul-de-sacs
and lanes?
Did they fight infernos in their gardens?
did that happen? just a while ago?
just down the road there?

I make sacraments to this quiet grey March morning,
God bless you, autumn, come
quickly, spread green, coax trees to life, soothe with your
sweet crystaline light, your
gentle sun, your brisk and
glistening air. Make things colder,
make it freezing, bring winter in harder
and wrap us all in fog and
frosts, turn lawn to ice, crack my
lips and fingers open with a litany of bitter cold.
I don't care! if its frezzing, if I freeze, if I
cannot leave the house for cold,
if the dripping tap
turns to ice in the night.
I will not once complain.
Just hasten that ferocious summer
hasten it gone gone
from all but memory,
and I will supplicate to sleet, to snow.

Learning Country

(From the Wilderness)

Back then
I stood amongst oceans of grasses
shimmering out and away endlessly
pale as silk and rustling,
unhuman waterless expanse in
thin light, hot acid lashing eyes.
The sky an excavation,
into furthest most pale blue.
And silence like held breath
waiting eons to exhale.
Only cicadas, and the wheedling bird
high up in the jetstream of thought,
dare challenge that great silence.
Not I.
I bowed, smote by that enormity
Of flat sky and vast flat
acres of pearly waving earth
whispering and flattening to winds
and amidst it all
I rose drowning
in the great silence
which was also a great flattening
a great cleansing
rinsing the air lit palely.

*

From the horizontal everything
one tree is a colossal rising.
God is in clouds in the mid-range,
high as the dogged transposed spire
of villages, the earnest facing off
of this utter flatness and silence,
the village profundity of brick and iron
the cross hung on staunchly
an antenna divining order, hope,
rains from prayers
bravely lifted into modest heights
of possibility.
Everything as the crow flies,
each red-dust road like bullish thoughts–
straight on, not one rise nor opposing view
to bend to.
Men are level-headed in the flat country.
Speak some, drink more, kill when necessary–
dogs and birds, beasts, bastards too
sometimes.

Women scan the horizon – for
hills, pods of brolga flying in from
the Kakadu, rainclouds, dustclouds,
disasters to break the uniformity of sky and earth
and grass and paddock, unfurled
at the foothills of Brobenah, Murrami, and
Stoney Point, Square Knob, Colinroobie,
gossamer country, blue hills, spirit country,

Big Rock Bunganbil country out there: maybe
a road smash, a bingle, maybe madness
and guns, somebody aberrating –
scanning for all this, with fear
and anticipation, people breaking
up, fucking, and going out into the
reddust country, out of their minds
into the greater mind, the big everywhere
unhitching the tethers of
sense and laughing loudly to echoing
Wiradjuri spirit of the big ancient
undertow; women
watching for deaths and
babies out of wedlock, even
suicide or just a limb torn off by the
combine, miscarriage – it
breaks the uniformity of days;
 mouths set against the Big Lonely.

One flip and we spin off the
rim of the earth, the lip of the sky,
and become eddies high up,
tiny shifting pinheads, in formation
of great birds – wedgetailed eagle, pelicans, brolgas.
Faith is in the fenceline, marking out
endlessness, the farmers tribute to
the possibilities.
I, smaller than a grain, a sinew of earth, a tree's
smallest parasite, some mortal insect
reduced to an essence in the simmering
of silence.

*

I couldn't Believe. My heart, shattered.
I fled from the simmering of the
ancient bloods and hatreds,
wastrel heat – murderer of babies,
elders and birds and stock. I,
ill-equipped to withstand
the awful scrutiny of
God there,
under seer light, the ancient
endless land, in the unrelenting
inhuman and magisterial silence.
Only the most humble can throw silence
back-crickets, throaty water falling
in brown channels, dockweed and thistle
and dirty dora, and dung,
that underlying wet smell
in evening light.

*

Then I grew older.
Time wrought a broken sturdiness within.
The vast sky and the flat
land revealed themselves
as my country, the weight of it all
drove me back to the
weighty blue
and fibrous rawcut rustling and
then I dropped in awe

before the horizon lit with blood
and the moon, the gouged out
socket of the night,
filled with the metallic creep,
amongst the endless land.
I was humble before the Immensity,
the utter unhuman finality
of such rustling yellow lands and
the crumbled red land and
the black land
I surrendered to the seas of wheat and
grass supplicating, and the
lonely giant sky.
I felt the imprint of it in my blood
and mind, felt blindly for it, tracing
my way back to Country, its
familiarity all I knew.
No longer afraid by light and heat
but curious and also
feeling the pull of all that,
out there,
in my own Wilderness,
to which I returned from
unspun.

Lost

Under the dry light we are clinging here
Brittle on the face of the land
A mere crust of us in cars and glass and bitumen
The bright false glitter and the smell of tyres and city
The fade of metal painted a uniform of colours
The uniform clitter clack of heels on footpaths and
Phones and creased foreheads –
The young buck talking behind gold shades.
It's all faraway car parks and the light filtered through
The dust of a dry March and the sky scalded and scarred
By summer fading, old wounds and whites smeared across the foreground
Old clouds like the reel might flicker and break off from the
Projector in a minute, the unutterable sadness of the 8mm
The quick movement of 70s kids in big print and seersucker
Dancing on coochgrass and under sprinklers rosy and rich with the greens and reds
Of cheeks and summer, a tumble and clutter of backyards
Everywhere, mums in short dresses. Beehived.
The faulty blur of the Past, back there,
In that dusty burr of light and filtered gold.
We are clutching here.
We are thin veneer, we are always on the surface of
The land and time, the present is deeper than
We can access.

Somewhere back there, are the quiet folk
All self-conscious and awkward to the pose
(People didn't use to know how to act in front of a camera).
It was formal.
Some just scowled, dead serious into the light.

Terry towelling and those polyester shorts and
Frocks – out come the plates of lamingtons, and scones,
The plates of sandwiches and the brown channel water washing the
 scene
In its wet babble, the red boat,
The guitar and the sideburns and bright pie and
The curl of an older barbie and the warble of magpies
And galahs squittering high up in the gums, ringbarked,
That sad deep smell of dirt, earth, soil, dust, ache,
It breaks my heart, all swept and gone away
How quickly does it all fall away,
And then

On this benign dusty afternoon
With the wind blowing up in the powder green of
Sad eucalyptus, along the corridors of footpaths, and the car parks
Through a din of dust and jackhammers,
The sky flung out in china blue, the faded, bleached
And lonely blue, the high heartache blue.

We are brittle there like sun-pilched plastic pots,
Worn beyond endurance, never present,
Always half-expecting to go. In the home country,
The roots and paths and mosses and stones of centuries
Bed down upon each other, the rhythmic incantation of days
Upon days, a dark green lichen-crusted gentle rolling erosion of
 time into time
Old people telling tales of the sea under the oil-lamps
And a thousands eons of poetry and ale.
The sound of stadium crowds the great roar of the ancient human
 spirits
Embedded and bedded there.

Here we toil under dust and make the noise of the club room
Of the cool shallowness of the air-conditioned bar
The mall, the cinema, all the brittle lights and spaces of no-culture,
Circulating ourselves through renovations and facades
Staying light and fruitless, staying unbound and hovering,

Whilst beneath and above and around
The dark red heart of the land rocks and rhythms,
The dusty ochre breath, the teardrops of the gumleaves
And the shrill call of the ancient birds and
The light, that dry godless light,
The filter of dust, the smell of caves
Of earth, of rocks and the still tall gum like a sentinel.
We cant reach it. We shy from it. We resent it, and when
It finds us we unravel.
It loses us. We cling on to the surface
And the roots unwatered break away.

We stay away from the core and root,
We walk with the wind blowing dust
And carry heavy burdens
Of unfed hearts.

See to Believe

You would not believe what I have seen.

I have seen cloud weighty as lead
Crouching lion on the rim of the Brindabellas
Full of impending winter.
I have seen a baby covered in blood and blinking, his cord uncut
From me; I kissed him bloodied and crying, an angel.
I have seen rosebuds filled with dewdrops
Opening slowly into spring sun.
I have seen children laughing and rolling in dirt.
I have seen my grandfather just before death, cry out to God.
I have seen my grandmother weeping for babies unborn.
I have seen statesmen lying, baldfaced, before millions,
And ordering youth to war for money,
For power.
Is this ignorance or evil? It has happened before.
I have seen a man broken by weakness and anger
Self-destruct and fall away.
I have seen truth unspoken in a look.
I have seen the sun rise as though it were the first day
A slow colouring of the world, a dawning,
A rising of bloodorange light, and all birds and dogs
Heralding the mystery of light with flapping and rattling
And joyous warbling and the rough bark and pant.

I have seen my children sleeping, with breath light and
Rhythmic, skin unimpeachable, foreheads uncreased,
Trusting me and the world in their deeply peaceful unconsciousness.
I have felt their hands upon my face and lips in
Mornings of sleepy warm joy,
That sprang from me, and from eternity, to warm me there
And fill my sleepy heart with gratitude.

I have seen mountains.
I have seen the sea,
And the sky like a vertiginous ocean above;
Completely new creatures, places, cultures, unearthed from the
Glorious Mystery of the world, discovered when all was thought to be known;
Headlines, amazement, when that which has always been known since
The dawn of time to be true, is proved-
The inhumanity of battle, the necessity of love, the evil of greed, the sanctity of life.
I have seen people sharing the last of their food.
I have seen people giving blood.
I have seen violence.
I have seen hate bloom like algae, watered by toxic tears of loss.
I have seen a million perfect things placed within our reach-
The perfect sustenance of bread, the light like honey, the water Divine.
Each of the millions its own small miracle.
To think that a moment of passionate chaos may bring forth life…
Or witness sheer strangenesses – chameleon, platypus, armadillo –
The magnitude of a tiger's symmetry, or dawning day, or stars.

I am mute with wonder
At all I have seen, and not,
That there is more to see
Than can ever be seen,
That these truths may be overlooked in a careless blindness,
Or worse, that they may be perceived and renounced;
That that which is known must
Eternally be learnt over.

www.ingramcontent.com/pod-product-compliance
Lightning Source LLC
Chambersburg PA
CBHW062140100526
44589CB00014B/1641